I0576307

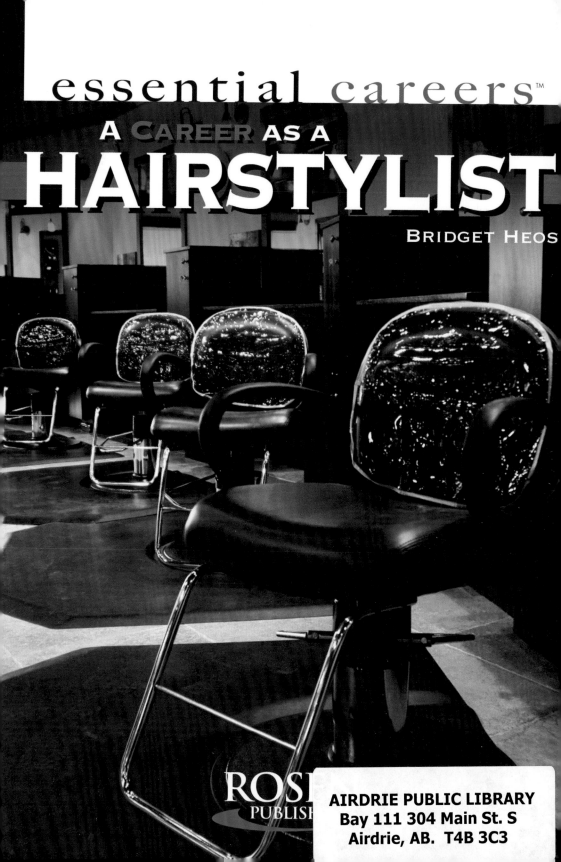

essential careers™

A CAREER AS A
HAIRSTYLIST

BRIDGET HEOS

ROSEN
PUBLISHING

For my mom

Published in 2011 by The Rosen Publishing Group, Inc.
29 East 21st Street, New York, NY 10010

Copyright © 2011 by The Rosen Publishing Group, Inc.

First Edition

Library of Congress Cataloging-in-Publication Data

Heos, Bridget.
A career as a hairstylist / Bridget Heos.—Cosmetology and barber school—Finding your 1st job—Succeeding in your 1st job—Career choices: hairstylist, barber, and business owner—Career choices: thinking outside the salon.
    p. cm.—(Essential careers)
Includes bibliographical references and index.
ISBN 978-1-4358-9474-7 (library binding)
1. Hairdressing—Vocational guidance—Juvenile literature. 2. Barbering—Vocational guidance—Juvenile literature. I. Title.
TT958.H46 2010
646.7'24023—dc22

                                                          2009047347

Manufactured in the United States of America

CPSIA Compliance Information: Batch #S10YA: For further information, contact Rosen Publishing, New York, New York, at 1-800-237-9932.

contents

INTRO

A career in styling hair lets a stylist help customers express their individuality and builds upon the creativity of the stylist as well. The possibilities are endless!

DUCTION

Are you artistic and good with your hands? Do you follow the latest styles? Have you styled your family's and friends' hair for fun? Most important, are you a people person? If you answered yes to these questions, then a career as a beautician or barber might be for you.

Beauticians, also known as cosmetologists, can work as hairstylists, barbers, aestheticians (doing facials), makeup artists, and nail technicians. This book will cover careers in hairstyling and barbering. Hairstylists cut, color, and style hair, and do chemical treatments such as straightening and permanents. Barbers specialize in haircuts and shaves.

Financially speaking, hairstyling is a sound career choice. Why? Because people will always want their hair done—even during a recession. Most people are unable to give themselves stylish haircuts, so they turn to a professional. If that pro is friendly and does a great job, then they'll stick with him or her for years.

Aside from economic stability, a hairstyling career allows people to provide an important service. There is a saying that "beauty is only skin deep," but the fact is, people feel better when they look good. That's why patients in hospitals and nursing homes are often given shampoos and haircuts by licensed cosmetologists as part of their treatment plans.

People usually think of beauticians as working in a salon, but there are other career options as well. These include selling cosmetic products or being a stylist for magazines, television, or movies.

Seventeen-year-old Kim Knox styles another teen's hair during a class at Nature Coast High School in Florida. Some high school vocational programs allow students to graduate as certified cosmetologists.

Whatever career path hairstylists choose, working well with people is essential. Just as no two heads of hair are alike, no two people are either. Some clients want to talk; others want to read a book during their appointment. Some describe specifically the hairstyle they want, while others are vague. Most of the time, hairstylists need to balance what the clients want with knowledge of what will look great on them.

Those who work in a salon or barbershop share close quarters with other stylists, who also have different personalities and senses of style. Getting to know clients and coworkers—and their unique hairstyle needs—is part of the fun!

chapter 1

COSMETOLOGY AND BARBER SCHOOL

Before you enroll in cosmetology or barber school, you may wonder if it's the right career for you. This quiz will help you decide.

1. How would you prefer to spend your day?
   a. Talking to others.
   a. Working quietly and independently.
   a. Half and half.

2. For how many hours a day would you be willing or able to be on your feet?
   a. Up to twelve.
   b. Four.
   c. Eight. "one on one"

3. Which schedule would you be happy with?
   a. Working the hours that are convenient for your customers.
   b. Nine to five, Monday through Friday.
   c. Making your own hours.

4. What is your view of beauty?
   a. When you look your best, you are beautiful.
   b. Either you're born with it or you're not.

c. Beauty is on the inside. It doesn't matter how you look on the outside.

If you answered A to all of these questions, then this career might be a good fit. You can also talk to your hairstylist or barber about their careers and ask if you can observe them one day. If you decide to pursue a hairstyling career, the next step is choosing a program.

Travis Thornton, a junior at Highland Springs Technical Center, won Virginia's high school cosmetology competition. Entering contests while in cosmetology school is a good way to practice hairstyling skills and gain recognition.

Some high schools have cosmetology courses or programs that allow students to take vocational credits off-campus at a junior college. Either way, students can be licensed cosmetologists by the time they graduate. High school programs can be judged in the same way post-secondary programs are. If it meets your needs, it would be a good deal financially. High school programs are not only free, they also allow cosmetologists to earn money a year earlier.

Other school districts and high schools may not offer cosmetology programs. And some students wait until after graduation to pursue this path. Those who attend a program after high school have several choices. The schools fall into three main categories: junior colleges, beauty schools, and barber colleges.

Cosmetologists and barbers are licensed by state boards, and schools are geared toward the requirements of their respective states. Students planning to attend school and work in different states should find out if they'll need additional credits. To find a cosmetology or barber school in state, go to the Web site of the state's cosmetology or barber board. (Sometimes they are the same.) When seeking schools elsewhere, check the Web sites of the National Cosmetology Association, the Beauty Schools Directory (which includes beauty and barber colleges), or area community colleges.

Once students have a list of possible schools, they'll want to consider several factors. First, will they attend barber school or cosmetology school? Both teach how to cut, color, perm, and style men's and women's hair. Barber colleges also teach shaving and business courses related to running a barbershop. In some cases, barbers learn skin and nail care. Cosmetology programs also teach manicuring, facials, makeup art, and waxing. Those interested in business courses related to owning or managing a salon might want to enroll in an entrepreneurial program at a community college.

Next, students will want to look at the program. How much hands-on training will they get? How often will they work on mannequins? Other students' hair? Walk-in customers? Is the lab up-to-date? How does the school teach customer service, people skills, business skills, and marketing? How does the school prepare students for the licensing exam? What is the passing rate? Does the school offer interview preparation and career counseling? What is the job placement rate? What is the student-teacher ratio? Who are the teachers? It's a good idea to visit the school to see if it is the right fit.

Students should also consider practical matters. If they don't have a car, can they take public transportation to the school? How much does the school cost? (When attending a junior college, in-state tuition is cheaper.) Students can seek the same financial aid through the U.S. Department of Education for cosmetology school as for a four-year college. Many beauty schools and beauty organizations offer scholarships specifically for cosmetology. At community colleges, general scholarships may also apply. Some schools also offer part-time programs, which allow students to work while attending school.

Check school Web sites for information on how and when to enroll and how to seek financial aid. Once admitted, students are in for a fun—but challenging—experience.

What to Expect in School

A full-time cosmetology or barber program usually lasts about nine months. Getting an associate's degree takes a little longer. Though shorter than a four-year program, days are usually longer. In a full-time program, you attend school from about 9 AM to 5 PM.

Besides providing beauty services, cosmetology students learn about health and hygiene. Students at Washington County Technical High School in Hagerstown, MD, display "germ farms" they grew, which taught them the importance of salon cleanliness.

The total credit hours needed vary by state. Usually, it's between 1,000 and 1,600 hours. They are divided into three areas: theory (learned in a classroom), lab (which involves working on mannequins or other students), and clinical (which involves working on customers).

Cosmetology school is hands-on. Far from being stuck in a classroom, students spend most of their time in the lab or clinic. Right away, they work on mannequins, soon after, on other students, and, finally, on customers.

Students learn how to listen to customers and how to practice safety and sanitation. They learn how to cut, color, style, perm, and relax all different hair types.

They also study people skills. For instance, in schools that use certain textbooks, they learn that there are four basic personality types: the executive, the caretaker, the fun-loving person, and the worker. They learn how to relate to each. The fun-loving client craves friendly conversation, for instance, while the executive focuses on the task at hand.

To some degree, they learn business skills, too. Because many barbers own their shops, barber students learn a great deal about this. Beauticians learn skills such as accounting, marketing, and customer service.

Finally, they practice the grunt work that hairstyling entails, such as washing towels and keeping your booth stocked and clean.

For textbooks, schools usually use ones published by Milady or Pivot Point. Let's look briefly at *Milady's Standard Cosmetology*. The book starts out with the history of cosmetology. It covers life and communication skills and personal image. It covers sanitation. Then it features chapters on anatomy and chemistry, focusing on skin, hair, and nails. Finally, it teaches various cosmetology techniques. In terms of hair, this includes shampooing, principles of design (such as which

Keeping a clean and well-stocked hair station is one of the lessons learned in cosmetology and barber school. Salon cleanliness helps prevent accidents and injuries.

cuts work with which facial features), and how to do different haircuts, styles, and treatments—such as the long layered cut, the French twist, and chemical relaxer treatments. It also teaches how to color hair and cut and fit wigs. At the end of the book, it covers business skills.

In the lab, students practice hairstyling techniques. Using other students as models, students experiment with different styles and colors. (A perk of cosmetology school is you'll always have a new hairstyle!) Often, students attend cosmetology school with the same small group of students. They become good friends. But they might also have personality conflicts. From this experience, students learn to see things from different points of view and to accept people as they are. It's not necessary to be best friends, but everyone should be treated in a professional manner.

In the hair clinic, students serve customers with a variety of hair needs. This is their chance to practice listening. The customer might say, "I want a short, layered haircut." That can mean lots of things. The student-stylists need to draw out more details or make suggestions. The customer might ask for a hairstyle made popular by a movie star. If that look wouldn't work for him or her, the student needs to say so tactfully.

TESTING AND MAKING THE MOST OF SCHOOL

It's important to make the most of cosmetology school. Arrive on time and stay on top of the details that make the day go smoothly, such as keeping a supply of fresh towels. Get to know professors, classmates, and clients. Join a professional organization, such as the National Cosmetology Association, Barbers International, or the United Barbers and Hairstylists Association (for minority barbers and hairstylists.) Take before and after photos of clinic work so that you'll have a portfolio to show employers. Visit salons to learn how they operate. Have a career

INTERVIEW WITH AN EDUCATOR

Anita Pankalla is the director of the Cosmetology, Nail Technology, and Esthetics Program at Johnson County Community College, Overland Park, Kansas.

How can you tell whether cosmetology is the right fit for you?
It should be something you're drawn to. You should be visual and creative and have a hands-on learning style. You don't have to be good at cutting hair right away. Some students pick it up quickly; others work and work and work. By the time they finish school, you can't tell the difference. Their work has the same quality.

What is your advice to students just starting out in cosmetology school?
No matter how frustrated you get, it is critical to practice, practice, practice. You cannot practice enough. It's not only how well you do it but also how quickly you can do it.

What is your advice to students who are starting their first job?
Know that you'll have to work hard and maybe a lot of hours—possibly evenings and weekends, and be excited about it. If you're bummed out, it will show. Be willing to pay your dues and be excited to help your customers and coworkers.

goal in mind, and know the steps needed to get there. Begin researching job opportunities while you're still in school. Meet with a representative in your school placement office regularly. Arrange for an internship. Keep in mind that finding a good job is a full-time job.

INTERVIEW WITH A STUDENT

Lindsay Robertson is a cosmetology student at Johnson County Community College, Overland Park, Kansas.

What is your advice for students just starting out?
You have to be a team player. If your classmates are running behind, help them, and they'll do the same for you. Being optimistic is a huge thing. If you doubt yourself, you'll never make it. Be open-minded. There are so many ways to do things, and there is so much more to learn than you think there is going to be.

What is your favorite thing about cosmetology school?
Learning with my classmates. We're all so different, and that makes it so much fun.

Toward the end of cosmetology or barber school, students take a written and possibly a practical exam, administered by their state board. The written exam is based on textbook material. Questions cover topics such as professional image, sanitation, properties of the hair and scalp, draping, shampooing, cutting, artistry in hairstyling, wet hairstyling, heat hairstyling, permanents, relaxing, straightening, coloring, and artificial hair. Specific questions may include, "How does the texture of hair affect the coloring process?" and "What causes a boring haircut?" Test takers are given four possible answers.

During the practical exam, judges observe students doing hair. They judge things such as if the test taker cuts the hair evenly on both sides and uses the proper techniques. These exams

Sarah Boyan, a student at Platt Technical High School in Milford, Connecticut, styles the hair of her classmate Dana Daniels. Cosmetology students begin cutting and styling hair right away, first working on mannequins and classmates.

are challenging, but schools prepare students with practice tests, such as the Milady's Standard State Exam Review for Cosmetology.

Once students pass the state board and graduate, their formal education is over. However, they'll be lifelong learners, staying on top of the latest styles and techniques—which is what makes the career so exciting.

chapter 2

FINDING YOUR
FIRST JOB

Prospective cosmetology and barber students will want to know whether new hairstylists and barbers are needed and how much they get paid. To see the current demand for these professions, check the Bureau of Labor Statistics' Web site. In general, the bureau says that as more teens and men get their hair done in salons, the demand for hairstylists will grow. The demand for barbers will stay the same.

The Bureau of Labor Statistics also provides information about the salary range of hairstylists and barbers. It gives the low average, middle average, and high average. Typically, an entry-level worker would earn the low average before working his or her way up to the middle or high average.

Those interested in this career should also talk to barbers and hairstylists about the outlook and salaries for these professions. Statistics don't paint the whole picture. For instance, some figures may represent only barbers or cosmetologists who are employees, not those who are self-employed. That can skew the numbers.

Maura Scali-Sheahan, director of education of Barbers International, said that she believes the demand for barbers is growing. She said that of the many barbers she has surveyed, the majority were in the position to hire new barbers. She added that as upscale and chain barbershops join the traditional neighborhood shops, the industry will grow.

Choosing a profession with job opportunities is important. It's also important to find a job you like, which hopefully will

Hairstylists and barbers can choose from a variety of work environments—from a neighborhood barbershop to a large salon or spa. That choice depends on the personality of the individual and personal preference.

lead to one you'll love. Your first step is to picture yourself five or ten years down the road. Where would you like to be? If you don't know, think about which classes you liked in school. Which did you like the least? What would be your ideal schedule? What would you like to do all day? Your dream may be career-oriented, such as owning a spa. Or it might be family-oriented, such as working part-time so that you can stay home with your children. Or it might be a little of both.

Whatever your dream is, write it down. Next, think about what steps will take you there. For example, if in five years you would like to work in an upscale salon, a first step would be to seek an internship or assistant position in one. If no such positions are available, you could still ask the manager for an informational interview. This is not a job interview. Instead, it's a chance to express your interest in the salon and find out what experience you would need to work there. This will point you in the direction of finding your first job.

Next, think about what you want from your first job. Are you willing to relocate? How far are you willing to commute? What realistic salary range are you seeking? Which benefits are essential to you? What atmosphere are you looking for? If you enjoy the excitement of weddings and proms, you might choose a salon that specializes in this. If you prefer a more laid-back atmosphere, a neighborhood salon might be best. If possible, visit the salon

Job hunters research work opportunities at the Job Center in Dayton, Ohio. While hairstyling is a recession-proof job, finding a position can still take a lot of preparation and legwork.

before you apply. Ask yourself if you would like to be a client here. Do the employees seem happy? Is it a friendly atmosphere? Are there red flags, such as bad sanitation, feuding employees, or an apparent lack of business? Chances are, your first job won't be your dream job, but it should be one that you can enjoy and learn from.

APPLYING AND INTERVIEWING

Typical places to find job listings include newspaper and online classifieds. Many cosmetology and barber organizations and Web sites also post jobs. Jobs can also be found by networking. For instance, a salon owner might e-mail her friends and family to say that she is seeking a hairstylist. If a recent graduate has sent an e-mail to his or her contacts saying that he or she is seeking a job, then they'll respond to the salon owner's e-mail with that information. Keeping in touch with classmates and teachers may also provide job leads.

A common first job for hairstylists is to work at a national chain or as an assistant at a salon. Spas, department stores, hotels, and even cruise ships may have entry-level positions open, too.

To apply for a job, students should write a professional-looking résumé. It should include information about their education, work, and volunteer experience. They'll also need a cover letter. This should explain why all of the above makes

Cosmetology student Kellie Meier highlights customer Kensia Harrison's hair at Minnesota School of Beauty in Lakeville, Minnesota, while teacher Angela Ericson looks on.

them good candidates for the job. The letter should be tailored to fit each job that is applied for. They should also have a list of references—teachers or supervisors that have agreed to give a positive recommendation.

When job seekers land interviews, they should prepare for the questions. Common questions include: Tell me about yourself. Why do you want to work here? What are your strengths as a hairstylist? What did you like about cosmetology school? What didn't you like? These questions should be answered honestly and positively. Bosses, teachers, and classmates should never be badmouthed in an interview. A positive answer to "What didn't you like about cosmetology school?" might be: "I'd been styling my friends and family's hair throughout high school. Relearning how to do that was hard at first, but I was excited to learn the right techniques." This shows that the job seeker saw the challenge as an opportunity.

Since interviewees are in the beauty business, they should look and act the part. A stylish haircut and outfit and manicured nails are important. Courtesy and self-confidence should be shown to everyone. The interview starts in the parking lot. The manager

Hair Innovator: Vidal Sassoon

Born in 1928, Vidal Sassoon grew up poor on the east side of London. When he was eleven years old, England entered World War II. Vidal and his family, who were Jewish, learned of the horrible acts the Nazis where carrying out in Europe.

When Vidal was fourteen, his mother dreamed of him in a barbershop. Believing it was a sign, she took him to Cohen's Beauty and Barbershop, where he worked as an apprentice.

Soon, Vidal changed his accent to sound upper class and left Cohen's to work in an upscale salon on the west side of London. Meanwhile, he joined a gang in his east side neighborhood to fight the British Union of Fascists, an anti-Semitic group. Once, he went to work at the posh salon after being beaten up badly the night before. When a shocked customer asked what happened, he said, "Nothing much. I just fell over a hairpin."

Vidal eventually opened his own salon. He experimented with new styles. In the early 1960s, he created the five-point cut, a short haircut that women could style themselves. It revolutionized hairstyling. Today, Sassoon is considered the father of modern hairstyling.

might be pulling in at the same time. Trying to beat her to the last space won't make a good first impression!

The interviewer will probably ask job seekers if they have any questions. Asking something shows interest and helps the job seekers decide whether the salon is right for them. (Job seekers are interviewing the salon, too!) If they are applying for a job as an assistant, they can ask what that job would entail. If they'll mostly be shampooing and prepping customers' hair,

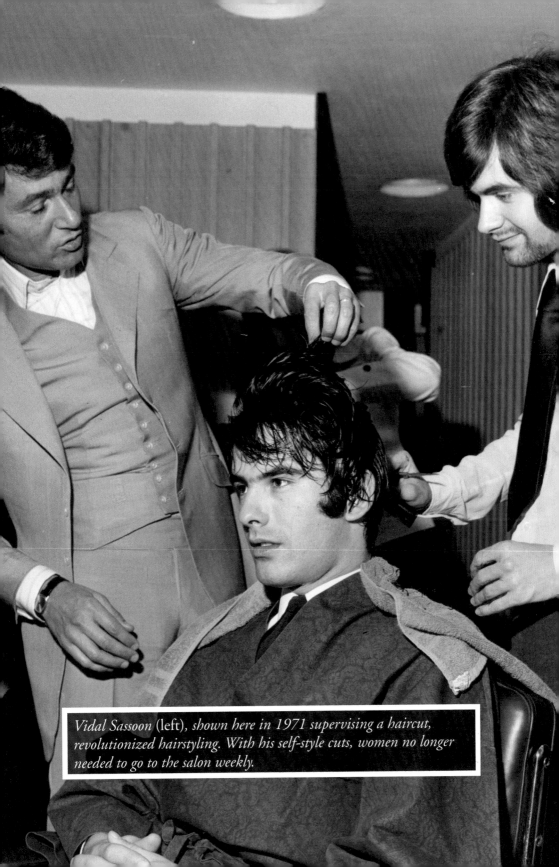

Vidal Sassoon (left), shown here in 1971 supervising a haircut, revolutionized hairstyling. With his self-style cuts, women no longer needed to go to the salon weekly.

they can ask if they'll get to style hair as well. Some salons set aside one day for assistants to take their own customers, allowing them to get practice and build a clientele.

Job applicants should wait until they are offered a job to ask about salary. However, they can ask basic questions, such as, "Are your employees paid salaries, commission, or both?" Salons and barbershops handle employee compensation in a variety of ways, including:

Ways to find hairstyling and barber jobs include networking and searching online job boards and classifieds. Networking helps to develop important contacts for the future.

- Salary or hourly wage only. Employees receive a steady paycheck no matter how many clients they have. Tips, of course, vary according to their number of customers.
- Salary plus commission. Employees get paid a base salary or wage plus a percentage of the amount each customer pays.
- Salary for hairstyling plus commission on hair products sold. This is the same as the salary or hourly wage–only model. However, employees also earn a percentage of the dollar amount of hair products they sell.
- Commission only. Employees may take home 30–50 percent of whatever clients pay. If there are no clients, employees don't get paid.
- Booth rental. Workers rent their space and keep whatever clients pay. Income is 100 percent determined on the number of clients. Workers pay their own taxes and purchase their own equipment. They are not employees.

Typically, first-year workers should not rent a booth or work on commission only. Without an established clientele, it's too risky.

After the interview, job seekers should send a thank-you note. If they didn't get the job, they should thank the interviewer for his or her time. If they did get the job, that's great!

HAIR INNOVATORS: ANNIE TURNBO MALONE AND MADAME C. J. WALKER

American women washed and styled their hair at home, often with homemade concoctions until the late 1800s, when many store-bought products became available to them. Two of the most successful products were created and sold by African American women.

Annie Turnbo Malone created Wonderful Hair Grower, a scalp and hair treatment for African Americans. Agents sold the product door-to-door. One such agent was Madame C. J. Walker.

Soon, Walker created her own product, which she also called Wonderful Hair Grower and sold door-to-door using agents. This became a multimillion-dollar company and provided a good living for its sales staff.

Both Malone and Walker opened factories, schools, and salons and contributed much of their wealth to African American causes. Today, Walker is the more well-known of these two entrepreneurs, but both revolutionized black hair care, creating many cosmetology jobs in the process.

Now is the time to negotiate a salary or wage. Starting out, barbers or stylists won't make a lot, but it should be a fair amount for an entry-level job. Also, employees should make sure they'll be working full-time with benefits, if that's what they are looking for.

Before signing a contract, it should be examined carefully. It should be understood before it is signed. Parents or people with experience in job contracts can help.

chapter 3

SUCCEEDING IN YOUR FIRST JOB

New hairstylists or barbers often take new or drop-in clients—people who don't have a regular hairstylist or are looking for a new one. In the course of a day, a mother might bring her one-year-old child for his first haircut. If he's scared or restless, he won't sit still. A homebound elderly woman might come in. Her only outings are to the doctor, church, and the beauty parlor. She's excited to be out and about. She wants a hairstyle that's not the new hairstylist's specialty, but the stylist will do his or her best. A teenager might drop in. She needs a prom updo, and she forgot to make an appointment. She's panicking.

These clients will each teach the new hairstylist something—whether it's about hair or people. These "one-time" visitors might also become lifelong clients. For instance, the girl getting a prom updo might usually have her mom color her hair. But if the hairstylist helps the girl with her prom emergency, she'll return for her next color job. As drop-in customers begin requesting this hairstylist, he or she will build a clientele.

A new hairstylist's or barber's schedule will likely include evenings or weekends. Days before holidays, such as the days before Thanksgiving and Christmas Eve, will be busy because people take off work and want to look nice for get-togethers. If

Prom, homecoming, and winter dance seasons can be busy times for hairstylists. Aubrie Rickford was one of 140 girls who had their hair styled on the same day for a school dance.

a hairstylist does prom or wedding updos, Saturdays will be busy, especially during spring.

While working, new barbers and stylists should learn as much as possible. They should stay up-to-date on hairstyling trends. They can do this by reading magazines and attending conferences and trade shows. At these shows, hairstylists demonstrate how to use products for the latest styles. To practice these, stylists can ask their salon manager if they can have a model night, where people volunteer to let cosmetologists try new styles on them. Workers should take advantage of any training sessions offered in the salon. They should learn techniques that help them work faster, allowing them to see more clients.

Much of what employees learn their first year doesn't have to do with hair. It's about people and communication. They learn how to make their clients feel comfortable by being friendly and positive. They learn to find out what clients want by asking if they prefer a big change or a trim, for instance. They learn how to tactfully tell a client that a haircut might not be right for him or her and how to encourage a client to try a new style that would be a good fit.

Sometimes, there might be miscommunication between a stylist and a client who doesn't like her haircut. The client might be angry. The stylist should keep his or her cool and offer to make adjustments. He or she can state his or her case calmly but shouldn't argue with the client. If the client wants to talk to a manager, she should be allowed to talk without interruption. After she has left, the stylist can explain what happened from his or her point of view. If the stylist truly made a mistake, apologies are a good idea. In this case, the manager might comp (not charge for) the haircut. Everybody endures difficult situations with clients. The important thing is to handle them with grace.

Hairstylists should be able to offer style advice to their customers based on the texture of their hair, shape of their face, and the time they spend on their hair each day.

Finally, a first job teaches the importance of good work habits. New stylists and barbers learn what they need to do to be on time and to look their best. They'll learn to keep an organized schedule. To be friendly to everyone. To work hard and pitch in when people need help. To keep their area clean and stocked. To make the boss's job easier.

A word about bosses: Most want their workers to enjoy and succeed in their jobs. However, if you have a difficult boss, consider you choices. Can you quit? If not, decide how you want to look back on handling the situation, and do that. The same is true of a job you dislike for other reasons. Determine if you can reasonably quit or if you need to stick it out for a while longer. In that case, set a timeframe for when you can seek a new job. That will give you something to look forward to.

Many barbers and hairstylists love their first job. But there comes a time when they want to earn more and challenge themselves with a new position. The next section talks about how to do that.

MOVING UP

With adequate experience, workers can advance from their entry-level job. They can do this at their present place of employment, by advancing from an assistant to a stylist, for instance. Or they can look elsewhere.

They might want to work at a more upscale salon, where they'll make more money per hair appointment. They may choose to work in a spa, which typically offers more services, including facials and massage, and requires its hairstylists to have more experience. Competition for high-end salon and spa work is steep. Job seekers will need to pound the pavement again, following the same steps they did to find their first job.

Spas offer additional services, such as facials, nail care, waxing, and massage. Finding work at an upscale spa can be difficult, but having prior experience helps.

But this time, they'll have years of experience, which will set them apart from other candidates.

Having a clientele is also a selling point to salons. For stylists and barbers working on commission, it's also essential to their income. If a clientele has been established, half of those customers will likely follow a stylist to a new salon if it isn't too far away.

But is the stylist allowed to take those clients from the present salon? When a stylist or barber is hired, he or she might have to sign a "non-compete" agreement. This states that upon quitting the job, the employee can't work as a hairstylist or barber within a certain distance (say 10 or 20 miles [16 or 32 kilometers]) for a certain amount of time (perhaps a year.) These agreements are meant to protect employers from losing clients that they invested advertising money to bring in. However, the agreement needs to protect the stylist's or barber's right to work, too. If a worker is concerned about the scope of a non-compete agreement, he or she should talk to a lawyer. The attorney may be able to negotiate a more reasonable agreement. Regardless of whether workers sign such an agreement, they are of course free to tell clients where they are moving and to ask clients to visit them in the new location. If a non-compete agreement requires workers to work several miles away, they might lose most of their clients. They'll have to rebuild.

In fact, for any hairstylist, building a clientele is an ongoing process. People move. They go to college. They try new things. Stylists and barbers need to replace old business with new business. To do that, they market themselves. Here are some ways to do that:

- Give clients two business cards. Ask them to give one to a friend. If the friend returns with it, you'll give both the client and friend a discounted haircut.

INTERVIEW WITH A HAIRSTYLIST AND SALON OWNER

Lori Underwood is a hairstylist and owner of Studio Lo in Kansas City, Missouri.

How did you know you wanted to be a hairstylist?
I was always interested in doing my friends' and sisters' hair and makeup. When it came time to decide on a college, my interest grew more intense. I ended up going to college for one semester and then decided to follow my true passion for hair.

What was your first job as a hairstylist?
My first job was an assistant position at a well-known salon and spa called Bijion. I worked there for one year.

What was your next career step after that?
I went to a booth-rental salon. It was a bit of a risk because I did not have many clients, but I knew it was what I wanted. So I worked very, very hard at becoming a booked stylist.

How did you come to own your own salon?
My husband and I bought a property a bit over a year ago with the intention of opening my own salon. I had worked for someone else in a booth-rental salon for over five years and was ready for the next step.

What does it take to be a good a hairstylist?
It takes a lot of determination. If you want to be good at something, you can be if you work hard enough at it. A good stylist has to keep up with hair trends and training. You need to make sure

your clients come first and do whatever it may be to please them. At the same time you need to steer them in the right direction to make sure they are looking their best!

What is your advice for those who would like to own their own salon?
My advice would be to be organized and professional, and make sure you have the best people working for you.

- Get involved with the local chamber of commerce and neighborhood business association. This is a great way to network with potential clients.
- Host a charity event, such as a cut-a-thon, in which hairstylists donate a day of haircuts. The people getting a haircut donate a set amount to a charity. This helps the charity and brings new clients into the salon.
- Cross promote. If a nail salon is next door, give the manicurist some of your business cards and take some of hers. You can both pass them out to customers.
- Send out mailings. Newsletters can feature new style trends and products, reminding customers to return.
- Send out holiday and birthday greetings.
- Use social media, such as Facebook and Twitter. Create a fan page on Facebook for people to join.
- Target specific clients. Younger clients are a growing customer demographic. Around prom season, advertise promotions, such as 10 percent off updos if two friends come in together. If there is a college near your salon, you may be able to attract students who haven't yet found a hairstylist in town. The school newspaper or online message board may be a good place to advertise.

- Run monthly sales promotions. Advertise these in your shop window, or if you can afford it, in a newspaper or other publication.
- Don't limit yourself. You should be able to do all kinds of hair: curly and straight, coarse and fine,

Marilyn Fling shaves Holland Houtz's head at Tim's Barbershop in St. Petersburg, Florida, before he begins a fund-raising walk. Participating in charity events is a great way to give back to the community—and bring in new customers.

thick and thin, natural and treated. You don't want to have to turn away business.

The most important part of growing your clientele is not getting new clients. It's keeping them. Give each client a great

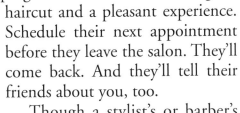

haircut and a pleasant experience. Schedule their next appointment before they leave the salon. They'll come back. And they'll tell their friends about you, too.

Though a stylist's or barber's second job is likely to be in a barbershop, salon, or spa, he or she might decide to make a major career change. He or she might sell hair products to other salons, do hair for magazines or television shows, or teach.

The following chapters will take a closer look at these careers—and the more traditional salon and barbershop jobs.

chapter 4

CAREER CHOICES: HAIRSTYLIST, BARBER, AND BUSINESS OWNER

Since ancient times, women have treasured beautiful hair. Ancient Egyptians wore weaves and wigs. Ancient Greek women dyed their hair red with henna or sprinkled gold powder on it. In Rome, elaborately curled long hair—often dyed blond—was the style. The slaves that did hair, *ornatrices*, were some of the first trained hairstylists.

In early America, women wore their hair long and styled it themselves. Then, in the early 1900s, women began opening hair salons. The need for salons grew in the 1920s, when the popular bob hairstyle required a professional's expertise. At first, some women went to barbers for bobs. Eventually, they opted for beauty shops, where they could also get permanents and hair coloring, manicures, and facials. With the growth of salons grew the need for beauty schools.

Both salons and schools were segregated at the time. However, careers in cosmetology offered both black and white women more independence and creative license than many other careers available.

In the 1940s, 1950s, and 1960s, the booming economy and popular hairstyles of the day brought beauty shops into their golden age. Bouffant hairstyles required weekly appointments. Then, in the early 1960s, Vidal Sassoon created the five-point

Since ancient times, people have relied on hairstylists to do their hair. This Egyptian wig—made of human hair—dates back to 1550–1300 BCE.

bob and other low-maintenance styles. Women no longer needed to go to the salon weekly. However, they continued to see stylists for haircuts and specialty services, such as highlighting, perms, and relaxing treatments.

Today, while segregation is illegal, many salons still serve either a white or black clientele. In some cases, this is because of neighborhood demographics and personal choice. In other cases, salons don't have stylists who can do ethnic hair. Cosmetology schools are trying to change this by teaching students to do all kinds of hair. They're teaching that hair doesn't differ so greatly between ethnic groups that they have to go to separate salons and barbershops.

Through the years, the styles and even the politics of hair have changed. But one thing has stayed the same: When it comes to their hair, many women trust only the pros.

Being a professional requires skillful hairstyling, which stylists learn through schooling and practice. It also involves excellent business skills, including knowing how to negotiate salary and fees.

Salaried employees will need to talk to their boss in order to earn more than their entry-level wage. They should always say why they deserve a raise (for example: "I've brought in x amount of customers in the past six months, and I average x amount of appointments a day") and not why they need it (for example: "I just moved into a more expensive apartment"). If the boss says no, employees can ask what goals they need to meet in order to get a raise. They should set a time to renegotiate.

When working on commission or renting a booth, workers can give themselves a raise by increasing prices every couple of years. Clients should be told tactfully when rates go up. Also rates shouldn't be raised too high or at the wrong time (such as during a recession). Stylists and barbers should be sensitive to their customers' need for affordable hairstyling, but they shouldn't sell themselves short either.

Weekly trips to the beauty salon were common in the 1950s. Women had their hair styled once a week and maintained the style until their next visit.

A third way to increase income is through product sales. Stylists who hope to boost their income this way should practice the art of soft selling. Tell the clients what you are using in their hair and why. Then, put the products in a basket at the front desk in case they are interested in buying them. Don't push the sale.

As stylists and barbers gain more business experience and a bigger clientele, they sometimes decide to go into business for themselves. This is a common choice for cosmetologists. About half are self-employed—either as booth renters or salon owners. You'll learn more about business ownership later in this chapter.

BARBERS

Barbers have a storied history. In ancient times, they not only cut hair. They also set broken bones and performed minor surgery. This continued through the Middle Ages. Then in the 1500s, King Henry VIII forbid barber-surgeons from doing anything more than pulling teeth and bloodletting—a process of removing blood, which people at the time thought cured sicknesses. By the end of the 1700s, barbers had given up dentistry and bloodletting and focused on making wigs, which were popular among men at the time. As wigs fell out of fashion, barbershops rose again. During and after the Civil War, they were a place to gather. In African American communities, patrons would sometimes sing together. This style became known as barbershop quartet.

Today, many men continue to gather at the neighborhood barbershops. Upscale barbershops and barbershop chains are leading to new employment options for barbers. And traditional neighborhood shops are being handed down to new generations of barbers. In a nod to history, the red-and-white pole symbolizes the blood-stained rags that barber-surgeons would wash and hang out to dry.

The Barber Surgeon, *a painting by artist Issac Koedyck, dates back to the 1600s. In those days, barbers cut hair and performed surgery.*

Nowadays, barbers are trained to cut, trim, and style hair and beards, as well as to do color and perms, but many just cut hair. With the dawn of the safety razor, shaving is less common. Barbering can be a solid career for the same reasons that

Many barbershops offer not only a haircut, but also a place to gather with friends and catch up on news. This inspires loyalty in customers.

hairstyling can be. Men want to look their best, and they turn to barbers for a good cut. Some men get their hair cut every month or, for a very short cut, every two weeks. Finally, men are often loyal to their barber and barbershop. They may return to the same place their whole lives and bring their sons, too.

Often, when barbers start out, they look for an open chair at a neighborhood or chain barbershop. They work for wages or salary in the beginning, rather than renting a chair. Eventually, many barbers go into business for themselves, either as a chair renter or as a barbershop owner. To achieve this, some barbers work for a barber who is hoping to sell his business down the road.

When barbers own their own business, they usually also cut hair. This requires them to handle the business end—accounting, purchasing, inventory, industry compliance, and human relations work during off hours.

The outlook for barbers is good. For years, upscale salons and spas catered to a mostly female clientele. Now, upscale barbershops (sometimes called grooming lounges) are offering men the luxury of spas with the masculinity of barbershops. Sports-themed barbershops, which advertise sports

INTERVIEW WITH A MASTER BARBER

Maura Scali-Sheahan is a master barber and an author.

How did you decide to be a barber?
I wanted to work with hair, but the beauty salon environment did not appeal to me, so I arranged to visit my father's barber. Within fifteen minutes of observing the barbers at work, I knew what I wanted to do.

Where did you attend barber school?
With the help of my father's barber, I was the first female allowed to enroll at the Chicago Barber College. The school was segregated by race, and once I enrolled, by sex, too. They assigned me a chair in the corner away from all the men.

What was your first barbershop job?
While still in school, I worked for the same barber who had helped me get into school. I did men's manicures chair-side, which means I did their nails while they had their hair cut. Once I graduated, I cut hair at the same barbershop.

What was your next career move?
I managed a shop in Georgia, then went back to Illinois and opened my own shop. I began writing articles for the *National Beauty School Journal*, relocated to Florida, and accepted a job at Florida Community College to start up their barbering program. An opportunity to revise the barbering textbook for Milady Publishing quickly followed and has continued to date, with my fourth edition of *Milady's Standard: Professional Barbering*

currently in the works. I now train educators and help barber schools strengthen their programs. I'm also the director of education for Barbers International. Combining interests and passions has led to great things and, as with any field, barbering has unlimited possibilities.

programming in a men-only atmosphere, and other chains are also breaking into the market. These places will create jobs and create competition. The neighborhood shop owners will need to work hard to bring in new clients and retain the old.

BUSINESS OWNER OR MANAGER

Many hairstylists and barbers work for themselves. A first step is often booth rental. This is a growing trend. It benefits hairstylists and barbers because they get their money on the day of service instead of waiting two weeks for the paycheck. It benefits salons because they do not have to pay taxes on tips earned by stylists (which go to the stylist, not the salon). It also requires less hands-on management.

In booth rental, stylists or barbers pay monthly rent to the salon or shop for space. Workers pay for their own health, liability, and short-term disability insurance. If they sell products, they acquire their own sales tax number. They keep track of income, tips, and expenses, and file their own taxes or hire an accountant. (It's best to set aside money quarterly for taxes but to pay in a bulk sum when it is due. That way, you accrue interest on your savings. Just make sure the money is there on April 15.)

Workers who rent a booth are self-employed. They cannot be required to work specific hours or days or to adhere to a non-compete agreement. Before entering into a booth rental, stylists and barbers should understand what they are responsible for and what the salon does. Will the salon owner market the salon, for instance, or are renters responsible for their own marketing?

Rather than renting a booth, some workers opt to work at home. This may work if their existing clientele lives close to their home, and if they have a quiet, clean work area available. The benefits of working from home are that there is no added rent, a percentage of rent or mortgage payments is tax deductible, work hours are flexible, and there is no commute. The disadvantages are that some clients prefer a salon atmosphere, and there may be distractions at home that make work difficult.

Renting a booth or working from home teaches workers how to order supplies, keep books, and market themselves. Those who would like to do that on a larger scale, while also managing employees and a work space, might want to own or manage a salon or barbershop.

Whether it's a small salon or barbershop, a large full-service spa, or a new barbershop or salon franchise, owners need business know-how. They might take online courses specializing in the cosmetology business, take general business courses, or work under a successful owner or manager.

Prospective owners will need to watch for opportunities. If they want to open a new salon in a certain neighborhood, they'll watch for rental space. In this case, they'll need to remodel the area to fit the salon or barbershop needs. An alternative is to buy a salon already in operation. In that case, the shape of the business should be assessed. Does it have a steady stream of customers? Will the hairstylists stay under new ownership? Is the equipment working? If not, can the business be turned around?

For workers wanting to manage a salon or franchise, their best bet is probably to get a job there and work their way up.

The responsibilities of an owner or manager include hiring, training, and managing associates. In any leadership position, it's important to keep employees happy. That's especially true with hairstyling and barbering. Customers are loyal to their stylists, not the shop. If workers leave, the customers go with them.

On the business side, owners and managers handle merchandising, bookkeeping, and marketing. They make sure employee paychecks go out on time and rent is paid on time. They might decide to have a partner. Sometimes one partner manages the employees and customer service while the other handles the business side.

When starting up a salon or barbershop, coming up with a name can be fun. Will it have a cheesy, pun name, a stylish name, or an old-school name? Setting up and decorating the shop and determining its atmosphere is also exciting. So is spreading the word and encouraging people to visit.

But starting a business is not all fun and excitement. Owners also need to work out rental contracts, remodeling expenses, financing, staffing, employee benefits, hiring, legal matters, and much more. Business ownership requires hours and hours of work, but it's rewarding to provide employment to workers and a service to the neighborhood.

chapter 5

CAREER CHOICES: THINKING OUTSIDE THE SALON

When stylists or barbers love their careers but no longer want to work in a salon or barbershop, they have lots of options. One is to work for a hair product company. These companies develop new shampoos, conditioners, hair colors, wigs, extensions, and other products for men and women. Jobs for one of these companies can provide an opportunity for travel and a more flexible schedule. Here are some jobs in this field:

Product Sales Representative. Sales representatives may work for the product company or a local or national distributor. These companies hire licensed cosmetologists since they are familiar with the products and the salon business. Sales people typically work on salary and commission. To break into the field, stylists can network with their salon's product reps. They can inquire about the field and let the reps know they are interested. Stylists can also go to trade shows and talk to representatives there. These meetings could lead to a job. Stylists should also pay attention to which products work best. Enthusiasm for a brand shows in a job interview.

Job hunter Bruce Edwards talks to Diana Nelso, an Avon representative, at a job fair. Selling cosmetology products is one career choice for hairstylists.

Product Educator/Platform Artist. To promote hair products, educators travel to salons and trade shows to train stylists. They demonstrate how to use the products to achieve the latest styles. They're called platform artists. To break into this field, stylists can assist another platform artist. They can also gain experience and notice by entering hair competitions. To succeed as a platform artist, stylists need to be good teachers and be able to project ideas confidently to a large audience. Typically these educators are not full-time employees. They freelance while working at a salon.

Schools are another place to work outside the salon. Teaching the next generation of hairstylists and barbers entails writing lesson plans; teaching hairstyling, safety, and hygiene; and observing students to ensure they have learned the techniques. Usually, one thousand to two thousand additional cosmetology hours are needed

Bobbi Harmon, who has grown her hair for twenty-eight years, gets her hair cut by Dee Ann Wallace at Bahama Mama's in Portland, Oregon, and will donate it to Locks of Love.

to be a cosmetology teacher. It's typically a 7:30 AM to 5:00 PM job, with evening homework to grade. Those who pursue this field find it rewarding to see their students master the art of hairstyling. In addition to teachers, cosmetology and barber schools also need program directors and curriculum developers.

Textbook companies—primarily Milady and Pivot Point—hire cosmetologists and barbers to write the textbooks used by schools. Stylists and barbers can gain experience for this by first writing articles for barber and hairstylist trade magazines.

Finally, there are niche jobs for cosmetologists wanting to do something different. One is working as a wig specialist. Many cancer centers across America have boutiques that include wig fitting and styling. This career allows hairstylists to help cancer patients—whether men, women, or children—feel better by looking their best.

Some stylists and barbers may want to broaden their horizons without leaving the salon. Volunteering is a great way to do that. For cosmetologists, there are lots of volunteer opportunities. Look Good . . . Feel Better is a service that helps cancer patients look their best. Locks of Love encourages people to donate their hair, which is used for wigs for children who suffer hair loss. Cut It Out trains hairstylists to recognize signs of domestic violence and encourage clients to get help. Through the Black Barbershop Health Outreach Program, barbershops that cater to an African American clientele can offer diabetes and high blood pressure screenings to their clients.

Both beauticians and barbers are needed by nursing homes and hospice programs to give bedridden or wheelchair-bound patients haircuts or shaves. This helps sick patients feel better in two ways. First, it cleans the scalp, making patients feel better physically. Second, it boosts patients' self-esteem. Their family tells them they look better. And they feel more like their old selves.

HAIR INNOVATOR: GUIDO PALAU

Raised in rural England, Guido Palau was a slacker in school. It didn't appear that he would make it as hairstylist either. He was fired from his job at a Vidal Sassoon salon. But he tried other salons and eventually worked as an assistant to a stylist. Soon, he was styling hair for catalogs and magazines.

He worked his way into the field of high fashion. Eventually, he styled hair for major runway shows by Marc Jacobs, Ralph Lauren, Versace, and others. Prada, Louis Vuitton, and Balenciaga hired him for their advertising campaigns.

Now, Palau is known for his over-the-top runway hairstyles. At the Spring/Summer 2008 Milan Fashion Week shows, he styled hair for the Roberto Cavalli and Moschino shows to look big, matte (not shiny), and cotton candyish.

In an August 2008 interview with the *Telegraph*, he said he wanted to go against the trend of shiny, glamorous locks. He added that women can achieve the look on a less dramatic scale by back brushing their hair for height (a popular technique in the 1960s) and using thickening products and baby powder.

Palau's runway looks have influenced hair fashions in the past. When he did model Kate Moss's hair for runway shows in the 1990s, he ushered in a decade of flat, smooth hair and ponytails. Because of his ability to both surprise and influence, he is one of the most famous hairstylists in the world today, as well as one of the most inventive.

CAREER CHOICE: HAIRSTYLIST FOR PRINT AND FILM

Stylists who want to work in an artistic, fast-paced, creative environment might consider being a print, television, or movie stylist. Print stylists work for magazines or catalogs. Fashion magazine work is considered the most prestigious of these. It involves styling hair for models appearing in publications like *Vogue* or *Elle*.

Stylists are typically freelance. They might work in a salon and moonlight as a print stylist until they are busy enough to be only a stylist. Typically, they get their feet wet by assisting a stylist. Eventually, they have enough experience to seek their own work.

They build their reputation by styling hair for models appearing in magazine fashion spreads. This is called editorial work. Next, stylists seek work as stylists for models appearing in advertisements. Advertising

Hairstylist Dominick Pucciarello talks to singer Mya during Fashion Week in New York. Hairstylists who break into the entertainment industry can style hair for runway shows, magazines, television, film, and other venues.

INTERVIEW WITH AN AGENT

India Gentile is an agent for stylists in Los Angeles, California.

Describe your job as an agent.
It is managing every aspect of an artist's career—from booking travel to negotiating rates, updating their portfolios, generating work, and establishing them in the world of beauty.

What are some of the most interesting projects you've worked on?
One of my hairstylists was chosen as the key hairstylists for Sarah Jessica Parker for *Sex and the City*.

What skills are required for your job?
Competence! Patience, balancing all the artists you represent. Being compassionate yet authoritative.

What experience do hairstylists need prior to becoming a freelance stylist for magazines, television, or film?
You need expertise at cutting and styling hair, as well as having basic knowledge of applying wigs and extensions. I would also recommend assisting one of your favorite editorial hairstylists for two to four years. Then build your book with tear sheets and when it gets to the point of you not being able to manage your jobs and work together, find an agency.

What skills or talents does it take to be a hairstylist for a magazine?
To work for a magazine like *Vogue*, you need ten to fifteen years of experience. For a less-established magazine, you may need only a few. You need to be a confident hairstylist and a good collaborator. You have to keep up with the trends, not just in hair, but also in fashion.

work pays much better, but the advertisers want to see editorial photos first.

The best cities for print stylists include New York, Los Angeles, Miami, and Chicago, but also smaller cities with strong advertising agencies, such as Kansas City.

Stylists interested in being print stylists can attend classes at well-known salons, such as Bumble and Bumble and Cutler Salon in New York. Working at a prestigious salon in their hometown is also a good stepping stone to a career in print hairstyling. Meanwhile, workers should study fashion magazines, learn who the key stylists are, and understand the style trends.

In order to find work or an agent, stylists need a portfolio. This should contain photos of a variety of hairstyles they've done. To create these photos, stylists can work with a photographer and model who are also building portfolios. If stylists have samples of work that has been in a magazine (tear sheets), they should include those, too. When the book is put together, the stylist can e-mail an agent stating that he or she is interested in assisting a stylist. The stylist should send a résumé and ask if he or she can send a portfolio. Once the stylist has gained experience, he or she can ask the agent for representation.

In order to keep being hired for jobs, stylists need to be talented, quick, and professional. They need to be on time, listen to what is needed, and, even if everyone else is acting stressed out, keep their cool.

Starting out, print stylists don't make much money. However, after several years, they can earn a steady or even lucrative income.

Other types of stylists work in film and television. These jobs might include being the stylist for a television show, advertisement, or movie, or for a particular actor. (Top actors usually have their own hairstylists on set.) Stylists are also needed for fashion runway shows, plays, ballets, and live television

Albie Mulcahy styles model Tracy Schaller's hair for a House of SKA fashion show in St. Petersburg, Florida. Mulcahy grew up poor in Boston. After seeing the movie Shampoo, *he decided to become a hairstylist.*

programs. Stylists can break into this field in the same way they would break into print media. In this case, they would likely need to live in New York or Los Angeles, though many ads are shot elsewhere. For a portfolio, they'll want to include a wider range of hairstyles, including wigs and period hairstyles. To work in Hollywood, they may also need to join the Makeup Artists and Hair Stylists Guild.

glossary

aesthetician A cosmetologist that focuses on skin care services, such as facials.

agent A person who represents an artist, such as a hairstylist, by booking jobs and negotiating contract and financial matters.

back brushing A process by which hair is given volume by holding sections of hair up and brushing it downward toward the roots. It is also known as back combing, teasing, and ratting.

barber A worker trained in haircutting and styling, and shaving.

beautician A worker trained in the cosmetology arts. Today, "cosmetologist" is the more common term.

beauty parlor A business that offers beauty services, such as hairstyling. Today, it is commonly known as a hair salon.

bloodletting The practice of removing blood from a patient to cure or prevent illness.

cosmetologist A worker trained in hairstyling, manicures, pedicures, waxing, facials, and makeup art.

freelance Describes a worker whose services are sold to buyers on a job-by-job basis.

grooming lounge A salon or spa specializing in men's services, such as haircuts and shaves.

hairstylist A cosmetologist specializing in hair care.

matte A dull (not shiny) finish.

Milady A company that publishes cosmetology and barbering textbooks.

nail technician A cosmetologist that specializes in manicures and pedicures.

Pivot Point A company that publishes cosmetology textbooks.

platform artist An artist that represents hair product companies by demonstrating hairstyling techniques using those products.

portfolio A collection of samples of a person's work, such as photographs of hairstyles a hairstylist has done.

print stylist A stylist that does hair for models appearing in magazine photo spreads, print ads, or catalogs.

salon A business that offers beauty services, such as hairstyling.

spa A business that offers beauty and relaxation services.

tear sheets Clippings from magazines that show an artist's work.

upscale Appealing to affluent customers.

for more information

Allied Beauty Association
145 Traders Boulevard East
Units 26 and 27
Mississauga, ON L4Z3L3
Canada
(905) 568-0158
Web site: http://www.abacanada.com
The Allied Beauty Association, formed in 1934, represents
  Canadian professionals in the beauty supply industry.
  It also hosts trade shows and competitions for hairstylists
  throughout Canada.

Barbers International
2708 Pine Street
Arkadelphia, AR 71924
(870) 230-0777
Web site: http://www.barbersinternational.com
Barbers International supports barbers in the United
  States by offering training, education, professional
  development, health insurance, and additional services
  and benefits.

Cosmetology Advancement Foundation
East 51st Street
New York, NY 10022
(212) 388-2771
Web site: http://www.cosmetology.org
The Cosmetology Advancement Foundation awards grants
  to cosmetology students.

Cosmetology Industry Association of British Columbia
899 West 8th Avenue
Vancouver, BC V5Z 1E3
Canada
(604) 871-0222
E-mail: info@ciabc.net
Web site: http://www.ciabc.net
The Cosmetology Industry Association of British Columbia
    is an organization for beauty professionals.

National Accrediting Commission of Cosmetology Arts and
    Sciences (NACCAS)
4401 Ford Avenue
Suite 1300
Alexandria, VA 22302-1432
(703) 600-7600
Web site: http://www.naccas.org
The NACCAS is a commission that accredits cosmetology
    schools that meet national standards. Its Web site
    also allows prospective students to search for accred-
    ited schools.

National Association of Barber Boards of America
2703 Pine Street
Arkadelphia, AR 71923
Web site: http://www.nationalbarberboards.com
The National Association of Barber Boards of America
    supports barbers and facilitates communication between
    state barber boards.

National Cosmetology Association
401 N. Michigan Avenue
Chicago, IL 60611

(866) 871-0656
E-mail: nca1@ncacares.org
Web site: http://www.ncacares.org
The National Cosmetology Association represents the interests of the salon industry. Members include salon owners, hairstylists, nail technicians, aestheticians, educators, and students.

Ontario Barber Association
510 Main Street E
Hamilton, ON L8N 1K7
Canada
(905) 547-6890
Web site: http://ontariobarberassociation.ca
The Ontario Barber Association brings awareness to barbering and new trends in barbering and supports barbers through education and training.

Professional Beauty Association
15825 N. 71st Street, Suite 100
Scottsdale, AZ 85254
(800) 468-2274
Web site: http://www.probeauty.org
A trade association that represents the interests of the professional beauty industry from manufacturers and distributors to salons and spas.

United Barbers and Hairstylists Association
422 E. State Street
Murfreesboro, TN 37130
The United Barbers and Hairstylists Association is a trade organization for minority barbershops and salons in America.

United Food and Commercial Workers International
    Union (UFCW)
1775 K Street NW
Washington, DC 20006
(202) 223-3111
Web site: http://www.ufcw.org
The UFCW is the union that represents barbers and beauti-
    cians, along with other groups of workers.

WEB SITES

Due to the changing nature of Internet links, Rosen Publishing
has developed an online list of Web sites related to the subject
of this book. This site is updated regularly. Please use this link
to access the list:

http://www.rosenlinks.com/ecar/hair

for further reading

Abecassis, Tally. *Barbershops*. New York, NY: Black Dog Publishing, 2005.

Barrett, Jim. *Aptitude, Personality & Motivation Tests: Assess Your Potential and Plan Your Career*. London, England: Kogan Page, 2004.

Biton, Davis. *Great Hair: Elegant Styles for Every Occasion*. New York, NY: Sterling-Penn Publishing, 2007.

Bolles, Richard. *What Color Is Your Parachute? 2010: A Practical Manual for Job-Hunters and Career-Changers*. New York, NY: Ten Speed Press, 2009.

Bradley, Laura. *The Brush-Off* (A Hair-Raising Mystery). New York, NY: Pocket, 2004.

Cohen, Nancy. *Died Blond* (Bad Hair Day Mysteries). New York, NY: Kensington, 2004.

Dickey, Anthony. *Hair Rules! The Ultimate Hair-Care Guide for Women with Kinky, Curly, or Wavy Hair*. New York, NY: Villard, 2003.

Ferguson Publishing. *Careers in Focus: Cosmetology*. 4th ed. New York, NY: Ferguson Publishing, 2008.

Flannigan, Annie. *Love and a Bad Hair Day*. New York, NY: Avon, 2003.

Gearhart, Susan. *Opportunities in Beauty and Modeling Careers*. Columbus, OH: McGraw-Hill, 2004.

Goodard-Clark, Lorri. *The Hair Color Mix Book: More Than 150 Recipes for Salon-Perfect Color at Home*. New York, NY: Harper Paperbacks, 2008.

Heckman, Marsha. *How to Cut Your Own Hair (Or Anyone Else's!): 15 Haircuts with Variations*. New York, NY: Black Dog, 2008.

Marberry, Craig. *Cuttin' Up: Wit and Wisdom from Black Barber Shops*. New York, NY: Doubleday, 2005.

Milady. *Professional Management for Men: Career Management for Barbers*. Albany, NY: Milady, 2006.

Morton, Rick. *50 Hairstylists*. Newbury Park, CA: Imagimedia Publishing, 2008.

Peterson's. *Teen's Guide to College and Career Success: Your High School Roadmap for College & Career Success* (Teen's Guide to College and Career Planning). 10th ed. Albany, NY: Peterson's, 2008.

Scali-Sheahan, Maura. *Milady's Standard: Professional Barbering*. Albany, NY: Milady, 2006.

Shamboosie. *Beautiful Black Hair: Real Solutions to Real Problems—A Step by Step Instructional Guide*. Phoenix, AZ: Amber Communications, 2002.

Vetica, Robert. *Good to Great Hair*. Beverly, MA: Fair Winds Press, 2009.

Worthington, Charles. *The Complete Book of Hairstyling*. Ontario, Canada: Firefly Books, 2002.

bibliography

American Salon. "The Way We Were." March 1, 2007. Retrieved Sept. 10, 2009 (http://www.americansalonmag.com/americansalon/article/articleDetail.jsp?id=410240&sk=&date=&pageID=5).

Arnesen, Eric. *Encyclopedia of U.S. Labor and Working Class History, Vol. 1.* New York, NY: Taylor & Francis Group, LLC, 2007.

Beatty, Kelly, and Dale Salvaggio Bradshaw. *Firestarters: 100 Job Profiles to Inspire Young Women.* Indianapolis, IN: JIST Works, 2006.

Bio.com. "Vidal Sassoon Biography." Retrieved September 10, 2009 (http://www.thebiographychannel.co.uk/biography_quotes/961:0/Vidal_Sassoon.htm).

Bureau of Labor Statistics. "Barbers, Cosmetologists, and Other Personal Appearance Workers." Retrieved June 14, 2009 (http://www.bls.gov/oco/ocos169.htm).

Charest-Papagno, Noella. *Cosmetology Specialties for the Bedridden Patient.* Hollywood, FL: J.J. Publishing, 1996.

Dennis, Mary. *Success Without College: Careers in Cosmetology.* Hauppauge, NY: Barron's Educational Series, 2000.

Ferguson Publishing. *Careers in Focus: Cosmetology.* New York, NY: Ferguson, 2003.

Gates, Henry Lewis, Jr. "Madame C. J. Walker: Her Crusade." *Time,* December 7, 1998. Retrieved Sept 12, 2009 (http://www.time.com/time/magazine/article/0,9171,989788-2,00.html).

Gentile, India. Interview. Sept. 14, 2009.

Hayden, Thomas, and James Williams. *Milady's Black Cosmetology*. Albany, NY: Milady, 1990.

IRS. *Cosmetology: Learning the Art of Doing Business*. Instructor's Guide. Washington, DC: IRS, 2004.

Jacobs-Huey, Lanita. *From the Kitchen to the Parlor: Language and Becoming in African American Women's Hair Care*. New York, NY: Oxford University Press, 2006.

Korman, Lorraine, with Felice Primeau Devine. *Cosmetology Career Starter*. 2nd ed. New York, NY: LearningExpress, 2002.

Lamb, Catherine. *Milady's Life Management Skills for Cosmetology, Barber-Styling, and Nail Technology*. Albany, NY: Milady, 1996.

Liotta, Alicia. "Vidal Sassoon: Living Legend." *Modern Salon*, Decemeber 4, 2008. Retrieved September 10, 2009 (http://modernsalon.com/ArticlesLandingPage/tabid/68/Default.aspx?tid=1&cid=17752).

Madame C. J. Walker: The Official Web Site. Retrieved September 10, 2009 (http://www.madamcjwalker.com/index.html).

Masters, Jan. "Guido Paulo: The Mane Man." August 3, 2008. Retrieved September 2009 (http://www.telegraph.co.uk/fashion/beauty/3365095/Guido-Palau-the-mane-man.html).

Milady. *Milady's Standard Cosmetology*. Albany, NY: Milady, 2008.

Nelson, Brett, ed. "The Fundamentals of Running a Beauty Salon." *Forbes*, April 20, 2007. Retrieved September 3, 2009 (http://www.forbes.com/2007/04/20/whole-foods-revlon-ent-manage-cx_bn_0420fundsalonintro.html?boxes=custom).

NPR. "Barbershop Quartets." March 18, 2002. Retrieved Sept. 3, 2009 (http://www.npr.org/programs/morning/features/patc/barbershop).

Pankalla, Anita. Interview. July 22, 2009.

Pivot Point. *Salon Fundamentals*. Evanston, IL: Pivot Point, 2000.

Robertson, Lindsay. Interview. July 22, 2009.

Scali-Sheahan, Maura. Interview. Sept. 14, 2009.

Tezak, Edward. *Milady's Successful Salon Management for Cosmetology Students*. 5th ed. Albany, NY: Milady, 2002.

Underwood, Lori. Interview. September 10, 2009.

Villa, Sam. "I'm a Cosmetology Platform Artist." *Modern Salon's Beauty School Advisor*. Retrieved September 10, 2009 (http://www.beautyschooladvisor.com/Industry-PeopleNote/I-am-a-Platform-Artist/cosmetology-platform-artist/260231/Default.aspx).

Wright, Crystal. *The Hair, Makeup & Styling Career Guide*. 2nd ed. Los Angeles, CA: Pace Publishing Group, 1994.

index

S

salon
    managing a, 52, 53
    owning a, 46, 52
Sassoon, Vidal, 26, 42–44, 59
Scali-Sheahan, Maura, 19–20,
    50–51
Sex and the City, 62
spas, working in, 35

T

teaching cosmetology, 56–58
Twitter, 39

U

Underwood, Lori, interview with,
    38–39
United Barbers and Hairstylists
    Association, 15

V

volunteering opportunities, 58

W

Walker, Madame C. J., 30
wig specialists, 58
writing textbooks and articles, 58

ABOUT THE AUTHOR

A former newspaper and magazine journalist, Bridget Heos is the author of several nonfiction books for young adults. She's had her hair styled in a barbershop, a spa, and her mother's kitchen. Now, she goes to a nice neighborhood salon. Heos lives in Kansas City with her husband and three sons.

PHOTO CREDITS

Designer: Matt Cauli; Editor: Bethany Bryan; Photo Researcher: Amy Feinberg